EXTREME JOBS

Astronauts

Tony Hyland

Smart Apple Media

This edition first published in 2006 in the United States of America by Smart Apple Media.

Smart Apple Media
2140 Howard Drive West
North Mankato
Minnesota 56003

First published in 2005 by
MACMILLAN EDUCATION AUSTRALIA PTY LTD
627 Chapel Street, South Yarra, Australia 3141

Visit our website at www.macmillan.com.au

Associated companies and representatives throughout the world.

Library of Congress Cataloging-in-Publication Data

Hyland, Tony.
    Astronauts / by Tony Hyland.
    p. cm. – (Extreme jobs)
    Includes index.
    ISBN-13: 978-1-58340-743-1
    1. Astronautics–Vocational guidance–Juvenile literature. 2. Astronauts–Juvenile literature. I. Title.

TL793.H95 2006
629.4023–dc22   2005056801

Edited by Ruth Jelley
Text and cover design by Peter Shaw
Page layout by SPG
Photo research by Legend Images

Printed in USA

Acknowledgments
The author is grateful for the assistance provided by NASA in arranging interviews for this book.
The author and the publisher are grateful to the following for permission to reproduce copyright material:

Cover photograph: Astronauts in space shuttle airlock, courtesy of NASA/Human Space Flight.

AAP/AP Photo/NASA, p. 8; Digital Vision, pp. 5, 12, 13; Getty Images, p. 30; Bill Ingalls/NASA/Getty Images, p. 23; NASA/Human Space Flight, pp. 1, 7, 9, 10, 11, 14, 15, 16, 17, 18, 19, 20, 21, 24, 25, 26, 27, 28; NASA/JPL/ Cornell University/Maas Digital, p. 29; NASA/JSC, pp. 6, 22; PhotoEssentials, p. 4.

While every care has been taken to trace and acknowledge copyright, the publisher tenders their apologies for any accidental infringement where copyright has proved untraceable. Where the attempt has been unsuccessful, the publisher welcomes information that would redress the situation.

Contents

Glossary words
When a word is printed in **bold**, you can look up its meaning in the Glossary on page 31.

Do you want to be an astronaut?

The booster rockets ignite on the space shuttle *Columbia*.

"10, 9, 8, 7, booster ignition, 4, 3, 2, 1 ... Liftoff!"

The **space shuttle** roars and shakes, and surges upwards. The **booster rockets** drop away. Within a few minutes the shuttle reaches Earth's **orbit**. The astronauts float in **microgravity** and prepare to carry out their tasks.

For most of us, this sounds like a dream. But astronauts and cosmonauts train for many years to do this. "Astronaut" is the term used by the United States space agency, National Aeronautics and Space Administration (NASA). It means "star sailor." "Cosmonaut" is the term used by the Russian space program. It means "universe sailor."

Astronauts and cosmonauts have an extreme job. They perform many different tasks. The commander and pilot control the space shuttle. Scientists perform experiments. Engineers launch satellites or repair damaged space equipment.

Does this sound like the job for you?

The edge of space

EXTREME INFO

How far is it to the Moon?
The moon is 238,850 miles (384,400 km) from Earth. The journey to the moon took about four days each way for the Apollo astronauts.

Shuttles travel to the edge of space and orbit the Earth. They orbit the Earth at about 120 miles (200 km) above sea level.

Shuttle astronauts only travel as far as Earth's orbit. Everything else in space is too far away to reach with today's spacecraft. Shuttle astronauts stay in orbit for about 12 days before returning to Earth. They work with astronauts from the International Space Station (ISS), or do other tasks such as repairing satellites.

The moon is the nearest place that astronauts could fly to. Between 1969 and 1972, 12 astronauts from the NASA **Apollo program** landed on the moon. Astronauts may return to the moon and even travel to Mars in the future.

The International Space Station with a space shuttle latched on.

5

Life as an astronaut

Astronauts spend most of their time on Earth, rather than in space. They spend years training for their space missions.

Astronauts have many jobs to do. They often help to design new equipment. Many astronauts travel to schools and colleges, talking to students about life in space.

Mission Control is the command center on Earth that controls space missions. Astronauts work here as **capsule communicators**. They talk to the crews in orbit about their daily activities and answer their questions. They understand the problems of living and working in space.

There is always work to be done at the Mission Control Center.

What do astronauts do in orbit?

Astronauts on a space mission are busy once the shuttle reaches orbit. They have less than two weeks to complete hundreds of tasks.

The **mission commander** and pilot take turns to control the shuttle. The other astronauts, known as **mission specialists**, have many jobs to do. Scientist astronauts set up their experiments and make notes. Engineer astronauts prepare to build sections of the ISS, or launch satellites from the shuttle's loading bay. When the time comes for the engineers to work outside the shuttle, other astronauts help them to suit up.

In their small amount of spare time, the astronauts keep the living quarters tidy. Even in space, someone has to do the housework.

Houston, we have a problem

The main NASA Mission Control Center is at Houston, in Texas. If something goes wrong in space, the experts here help the astronauts to find a solution.

Scientist astronauts carefully set up experiments on board the shuttle.

Risks and dangers

There are many risks and dangers for astronauts. Humans cannot survive in space without proper equipment and training. The astronauts' training and equipment reduce the risks and dangers they face in space. Some of the risks for astronauts are:

Losing air   There's no air in space. Each shuttle carries enough air for the crew for the entire trip. Shuttles and spacesuits are tightly sealed to hold air in.

Temperature   The **temperature** in space depends on sunlight. In the sunlight, the temperature reaches 250°F (120°C). Out of the sun, the temperature drops to −240°F (−150°C).

Radiation   Space is filled with dangerous **radiation**, such as X rays and gamma rays. Suits and shuttles must be shielded from radiation.

Explosion   The shuttle's booster rockets burn like huge firecrackers. If anything goes wrong, they can explode. In 1986, the shuttle *Challenger* exploded 73 seconds after launch, killing the crew.

The shuttle *Challenger* exploded shortly after launch.

Airtight

Spacecraft are sealed tightly so that no air is lost into space. If there is a leak in the spacecraft, air will squirt through the hole and disappear into space. Astronauts can't afford to let their breathing air escape into space.

When astronauts need to work outside the spacecraft, they first enter a room called an airlock. The room is sealed shut. Air is pumped out of the airlock. Then the outside door opens and the astronauts float outside. Little precious air escapes into space.

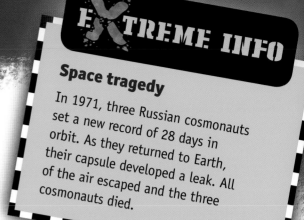

Astronauts put their suits on before the air is pumped out of the airlock.

Training

Astronauts train for at least two years before they go into space. Even experienced astronauts practice their skills over and over.

Pilot astronauts must be experienced military jet pilots. Other astronauts are usually either scientists or engineers. All astronauts need to be very fit and healthy.

All trainee astronauts have already studied mathematics and science. As trainees, they learn more about the science of space flight, including astronomy, navigation, and the systems inside the shuttle. Surprisingly, one of the first things trainee astronauts learn is scuba diving. This allows them to train underwater in the **Neutral Buoyancy Lab**. They spend many hours in the Neutral Buoyancy Lab wearing spacesuits to experience the feeling of weightlessness.

NASA astronauts also learn Russian so they can communicate with Russian cosmonauts on the ISS.

Astronauts train for weightlessness underwater in the Neutral Buoyancy Lab.

Simulators

Astronauts do much of their training in simulators. These are exact copies of the real shuttles and their equipment. The simulators use computers to imitate taking off, flying, and landing. Astronauts can practice their tasks over and over, until they know them perfectly. Pilot astronauts must keep their flying skills sharp. They also spend many hours each month flying jet trainers to practice navigation, take-offs, and landings.

To get used to microgravity, trainee astronauts travel in a special plane that makes repeated dives in midair. Each dive gives the astronauts a feeling of weightlessness for about 20 seconds.

EXTREME INFO

The oldest astronaut

In 1961, John Glenn was the first U.S. astronaut to go into orbit. In 1998, he went into space again, this time aboard the space shuttle. He was 77 years old.

Astronauts learn the feeling of weightlessness in a special plane.

Astronauts in history

In the 1950s and 1960s, the U.S. and the Union of Soviet Socialist Republics (now Russia) competed fiercely to achieve the most in space. This is often called the "space race."

The first person to fly in space was the Russian cosmonaut Yuri Gagarin. He flew into orbit in 1961. The first American astronauts flew a few months later. Alan Shepard flew into space for just 15 minutes. Later that year, John Glenn became the first American to go into orbit.

In 1969, astronauts Neil Armstrong and Edwin Aldrin landed on the moon in a small spacecraft. They started the journey back to Earth a few hours later. Several more **expeditions** went to the moon. Astronauts even drove around on the moon in a "moon buggy." The last expedition to the moon was in 1972.

NASA astronauts first walked on the moon in 1969.

Shuttles and space stations

Space shuttles can fly into space and return many times. NASA launched the first space shuttle, *Columbia*, in 1982. Since then, five shuttles have made over a hundred flights into orbit.

Astronauts use the shuttles to perform many tasks. They carry new satellites into orbit and retrieve old ones. They carry parts for the ISS, and transport the astronauts who will stay and work there.

The earliest space stations were the Russian *Soyuz* and the American *Skylab*. They were tiny and cramped, but people lived on them for weeks at a time. Today, astronauts live and work on the ISS for about six months.

EXTREME INFO

Shuttle tragedies

Two shuttle flights have ended in tragedy. In 1986, the shuttle *Challenger* exploded just after liftoff. In 2003, the shuttle *Columbia* broke apart while reentering Earth's atmosphere.

The space shuttles can be hooked up to the ISS.

Astronaut jobs

Shuttle pilots

Shuttles have two pilots—the mission commander and a copilot. The pilots' main job is to fly the shuttle, both **maneuvering** in orbit and flying back to Earth.

In orbit, the pilots maneuver the shuttle by firing the control jets in brief spurts. The shuttle moves slowly up to the space station airlock so that astronauts can transfer safely.

At the end of the mission, the pilots fly the shuttle back to Earth. The pilots' task is to move the ship into position, then drop out of orbit. The shuttle encounters intense heat as it enters the atmosphere. Once the shuttle is past this stage, it glides in to land with the pilot in control.

The mission commander and pilot control the shuttle from the flight deck.

PROFILE

Duane Carey

Shuttle pilot

Duane Carey studies a manual aboard the shuttle *Columbia*.

Job

In 2002, I flew as a copilot on shuttle mission STS-109, flying the shuttle *Columbia*.

Experience

I was an Air Force test pilot, flying F-16 jets. I had spent over 3,500 hours flying jets before I became an astronaut in 1996.

Career highlight

On my shuttle mission, we fitted new equipment to the Hubble Space Telescope. It was a difficult job that took five days of **spacewalks**.

Most exciting moment

Those first few minutes of liftoff, as the shuttle accelerates. There is a terrific shaking, and you feel a tremendous pushing sensation.

How I became an astronaut

When I left school I didn't know what I wanted to do. After traveling around the country for a few years, I set my sights on becoming an astronaut. I studied **aerospace engineering**, then became an Air Force pilot, and eventually an astronaut.

RISK FACTOR

Pilot astronauts are skilled and experienced. There are risks in their work, such as:

- catastrophic explosions
- colliding with the space station
- misjudging reentry angles

Engineers

Engineers are experts in building things and controlling machinery. Engineer astronauts control the **robotic arm** on the shuttle and space station.

Every shuttle flight has one main task. The astronauts may be launching a satellite, or building a new section of the ISS. The astronauts who do spacewalks are engineers. They work outside the shuttle in spacesuits for up to seven hours at a time. Their work is difficult. The bulky suits are awkward to work in and the gloves make it hard to grip tools. Even using a wrench or a drill is slow and difficult.

The engineers cannot carry checklists outside the shuttle. Another astronaut, often the pilot, uses a checklist to direct the engineers from inside the shuttle.

An engineer works on the robotic arm on the ISS.

PROFILE

Stephanie Wilson

Engineer

Job

I'm a mission specialist engineer.

Stephanie Wilson in training for her future space mission.

Experience

I worked as an aerospace engineer, then started astronaut training in 1996. I've worked in Mission Control, and the Shuttle and Station Operations branches. I expect to fly to space in 2007.

Training

Training is interesting and exciting. I could be flying, or diving in the Neutral Buoyancy Lab. I can be operating the robotic arm, or learning to speak Russian. I'm never bored.

My future

I want to fly on a shuttle. Eventually, I hope to live and work on the ISS for six months.

Why I became an astronaut

When I was young I wanted to be an astronomer. Later, I became an aerospace engineer. I joined NASA because I wanted to be involved in designing missions to send astronauts into space.

RISK FACTOR

Engineer astronauts have a difficult job. They face risks, such as:

- spacesuit failure
- being injured while working in space

Astronaut jobs

Scientists

Some scientist astronauts are medical doctors. Others are experts in **chemistry, biology**, and other sciences. Scientist astronauts perform experiments to gain new scientific knowledge.

Scientists want to learn many things that can only be discovered in space. The scientist astronauts perform many experiments as they orbit Earth. One experiment observed how spiders spin their webs in microgravity. Scientists also observe how plants grow in microgravity. This could be important in the future for astronauts on a long space voyage who want to grow fresh food on their journey.

Scientist astronauts can set up scientific instruments outside the space station to record temperature or to gather data about the sun.

EXTREME INFO

Long voyage

If astronauts travel to Mars, the trip will take many months each way. Scientists look for ways to make sure that the astronauts will still be fit and healthy when they arrive.

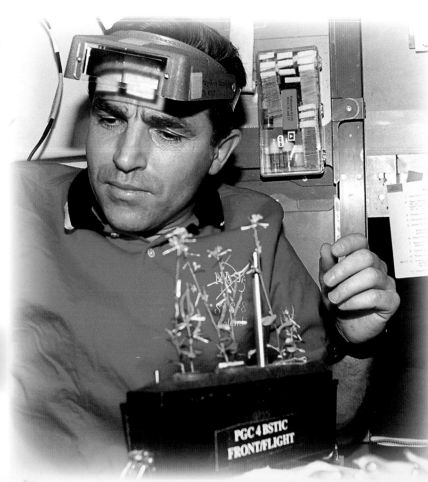

A scientist performs an experiment in the space shuttle.

18

The human body in space

Living in space is hard on the human body. Without gravity, body fluids are not pulled towards the feet, so the astronauts' faces swell a little. Muscles become weaker because they are not being used to hold the body up. Normal exercise strengthens our bones. But astronauts lose calcium from their bones because they cannot exercise properly in microgravity. This could lead to problems on a long space voyage.

Scientist astronauts can measure the effects of space travel on humans. They test exercise programs and diets, to see which exercises and food help the most. Their experiments will help future astronauts to live more safely in space.

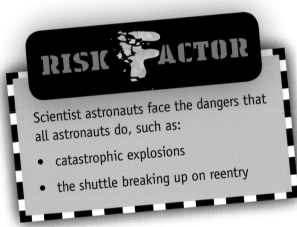

RISK FACTOR

Scientist astronauts face the dangers that all astronauts do, such as:

- catastrophic explosions
- the shuttle breaking up on reentry

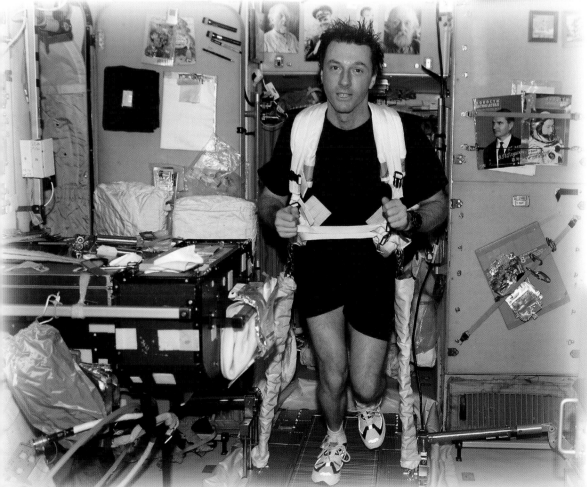

An astronaut must be firmly strapped to the treadmill when exercising in microgravity.

19

Astronaut jobs

Mission commanders

Mission commanders are experienced shuttle pilots who have flown several times as a copilot. Most shuttle pilots worked as military pilots before they began astronaut training.

Once the shuttle is in orbit, the mission commander has many duties to perform. The most important duties are flying the shuttle to meet the space station or launching a satellite. This takes very careful maneuvering.

The mission commander makes sure that the other specialists have time to do their jobs. This sometimes means lending a helping hand, or just taking over the cleaning. When the mission is over, the commander takes charge of flying the shuttle back to Earth.

The mission commander gently maneuvers the shuttle when approaching the space station.

PROFILE

Pamela Melroy

Shuttle pilot

Pamela Melroy is an experienced NASA space shuttle pilot.

Job

I've flown as a pilot on two shuttle missions. I hope to be mission commander next time.

Experience

I was an Air Force pilot in the Persian Gulf War in 1991. Then I became a test pilot. On my shuttle missions we helped to construct the ISS.

Career highlight

When the shuttle landed at the end of my first mission, I knew that I'd played my part in a difficult but successful mission.

Scariest moment

After I had suited up two spacewalkers and checked their spacesuits and connections, I turned the valve on the airlock to pump out the air. I knew that if I hadn't done my job properly, something very bad would happen.

Why I'm an astronaut

Seeing astronauts step onto the moon inspired me to become an astronaut. Exploring our solar system is a gift that I can give to our community.

Pamela Melroy at the controls of the space shuttle.

RISK FACTOR

Mission commanders are responsible for the safety of the shuttle. The risks they face include:

- catastrophic explosions
- losing control of the shuttle
- crash landing

21

Astronaut jobs

Teachers in space

Children want to learn about space. Who could teach them better than teachers who have been there?

NASA's newest astronauts are not pilots or scientists, but experienced schoolteachers. They are known as educator astronauts. They can explain to students what it's like to be an astronaut. They can work with other teachers to design lessons for children all over the world.

Educator astronauts have to be fit and healthy, and interested in space. However, they do not need a strong background in science and mathematics like other astronauts. The most important requirement is that they are excellent, interesting teachers.

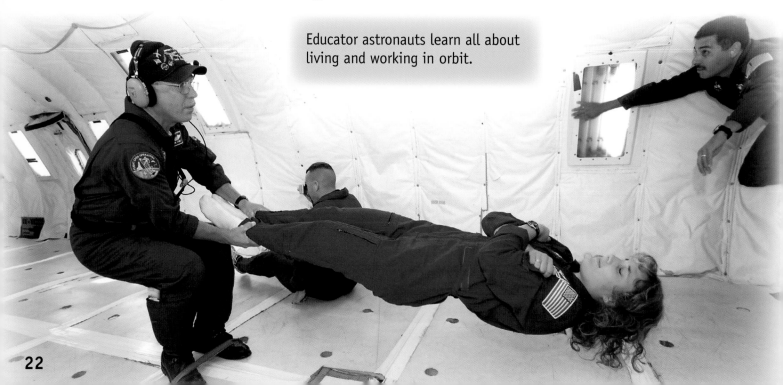

Educator astronauts learn all about living and working in orbit.

Educators at work

Educator astronauts do the same two-year training course as other astronauts. This includes survival training, T-38 jet training, and practicing tasks on the shuttle simulators. After that, they travel into space and do the same work that other astronauts do. They travel in the shuttle and live on the ISS. They perform spacewalks and carry out science experiments. When they return to Earth, they spend much of their time working in schools, teaching children about life in orbit.

Perhaps one day those children will become astronauts themselves. Others may become scientists or engineers. There are many jobs in the space program besides astronauts.

RISK FACTOR

Educator astronauts face the same risks as all astronauts, including:

- the dangers of launches and landings
- accidents in space
- spacesuit failure

Educator astronauts work with a group of children.

International astronauts

Most of the NASA astronauts are American citizens. However, astronauts from countries such as Australia, Canada, and Japan have worked on shuttles or the ISS as mission specialists.

India's first astronaut, Kalpana Chawla, flew on two shuttle missions as a mission specialist. She was killed when *Columbia* broke up in 2003. Ilan Ramon, the first Israeli astronaut, was also killed in the *Columbia* accident. He was also a mission specialist. China has sent astronauts into orbit in a small capsule like the Russian and early American spacecraft. Other countries may send astronauts into space in the future.

The crew of the ISS are usually a mix of NASA astronauts and Russian cosmonauts. Sometimes the European Space Agency (ESA) sends an astronaut to the ISS.

EXTREME INFO

First woman in space

Cosmonaut Valentina Tereshkova was the first woman to fly into space, in 1963. The first American woman was Sally Ride, in 1983. Today, many women have flown as astronauts.

NASA astronaut Peter Wisoff works with Japanese astronaut Koichi Wakata on a shuttle.

Russian cosmonauts

During the early years of the space race, Russian cosmonauts set many records for staying in space for long periods. The longest stay in space was 438 days. The record was set by Valeri Polyakov.

For many years, Russia and the U.S. have worked together on space programs. Many Russian cosmonauts have flown in NASA shuttles. ISS crews are usually a mix of Russians and Americans, with astronauts from other countries staying as well.

Russia does not have a reusable spacecraft like the shuttle. Instead, cosmonauts fly to and from the ISS in a craft which parachutes back to Earth. The unmanned section of the craft burns up as it reaches the atmosphere.

Russian cosmonaut Yuri Onufrienko working on the ISS.

RISK FACTOR

Many of the Russian cosmonauts spend long periods in the ISS. There, they face risks, such as:

- serious illness or injury, which cannot be treated in space
- prolonged exposure to space radiation
- serious meteorite damage to the ISS

Living in space

Astronauts need to eat, sleep, breathe, and keep clean and healthy in space. But these things are difficult to do in microgravity.

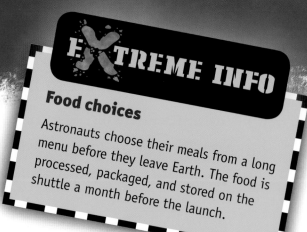
Astronauts float freely in a shuttle or space station, and so does all of their equipment. Velcro keeps equipment in place. Astronauts sometimes sleep in sleeping bags stuck to the wall with velcro.

Food and drink can be tricky to deal with. Food is kept in single-serve packages. Much of the food is sticky, so that bits won't float away. The astronauts drink from containers with lids or straws.

Washing is also difficult in microgravity. Showers do not work well. Instead, astronauts wash with a damp cloth.

The food that astronauts eat in space is pre-packaged on Earth before the voyage.

Leisure time

Astronauts have some leisure time in between completing their mission tasks. One favorite pastime is gazing out the window, enjoying the spectacular views of Earth.

Astronauts often find quiet pastimes such as reading, listening to music, or taking photos. Spare time is a good time to speak to family members on Earth, or to answer e-mail.

Exercise is important. Astronauts work out on a treadmill or an exercise bike for about two hours a day. On the space station, astronauts sometimes play a game of microgravity tag, chasing each other through the various sections.

Astronauts enjoy playing and listening to music in their leisure time.

The future in space

For the near future, astronauts will only travel to Earth's orbit. Eventually, shuttles will be replaced by newer and better spacecraft.

As we reach further into space, we will need more astronauts with a much wider range of skills. The Apollo astronauts simply traveled to the moon and returned. By 2020 astronauts will probably return to the moon to set up large, permanent bases. They will live and work on the moon for long periods. They will explore the moon, searching for useful minerals.

The moon would be a handy launching place for expeditions further into space. Its low gravity would make it easier for rockets to launch large space vehicles.

EXTREME INFO

Robots in space

Before humans return to the moon, robots will go there. They will explore the surface in preparation for the first bases for humans.

NASA will send robots to explore the moon in the future.

To Mars and beyond

Mars is the nearest planet to Earth.
Expeditions to Mars could start by the
year 2020. Astronauts would explore Mars and set up
permanent bases. In the future, colonies of humans
might live on Mars. Some of the moons of Jupiter and
Saturn are rather like Mars. Astronauts could also travel
to these moons.

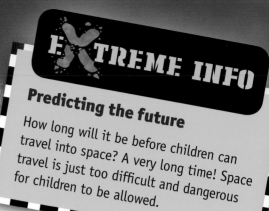

EXTREME INFO

Predicting the future

How long will it be before children can travel into space? A very long time! Space travel is just too difficult and dangerous for children to be allowed.

Millions of asteroids circle the sun in the **asteroid belt.**
One day, astronauts might explore the asteroid belt.

Alpha Centauri is the nearest star to our solar
system. Alpha Centauri is so far away that its
light takes over four years to reach us. A
human expedition to Alpha Centauri would
take hundreds of years. Unless scientists of
the future can invent much faster space travel,
humans may never travel beyond our
solar system.

The Mars Exploration
Rover has been sent
to Mars to carry out
research.

Could you be an astronaut?

You could be an astronaut if you:

- do well in school

- study maths and science in school

- go to college and study science, maths, or engineering

- work in your field after college

- are very fit and healthy, and have good eyesight.

If you want to be a shuttle pilot, you'll need to train as a jet pilot first.

Studying science at school is a good place to start if you want to be an astronaut.

Glossary

aerospace engineering	the design of spacecraft
Apollo program	the NASA program to land astronauts on the moon
asteroid belt	a large area of small planets found between Mars and Jupiter
biology	the branch of science that deals with living things
booster rockets	large extra rockets that push the space shuttle near to orbit
capsule communicators	people trained to speak to astronauts in space
chemistry	the branch of science that deals with chemicals and substances
expeditions	journeys made for a purpose; missions
maneuvering	moving something carefully and skillfully
microgravity	the sensation of near-weightlessness experienced in orbit
mission commander	commander of any space shuttle mission
Mission Control	the control headquarters for all shuttle and International Space Station missions
mission specialists	astronauts trained for a specific mission
Neutral Buoyancy Lab	a large pool, designed to give astronauts a sensation of weightlessness
orbit	the path of a satellite around a larger body such as Earth
radiation	harmful rays, such as X rays and gamma rays
robotic arm	a large mechanical arm, controlled by astronauts
space shuttle	a reusable spacecraft
spacewalks	when astronauts go outside the space shuttle to carry out work on satellites or the International Space Station
temperature	the amount of heat in a body or object

Index